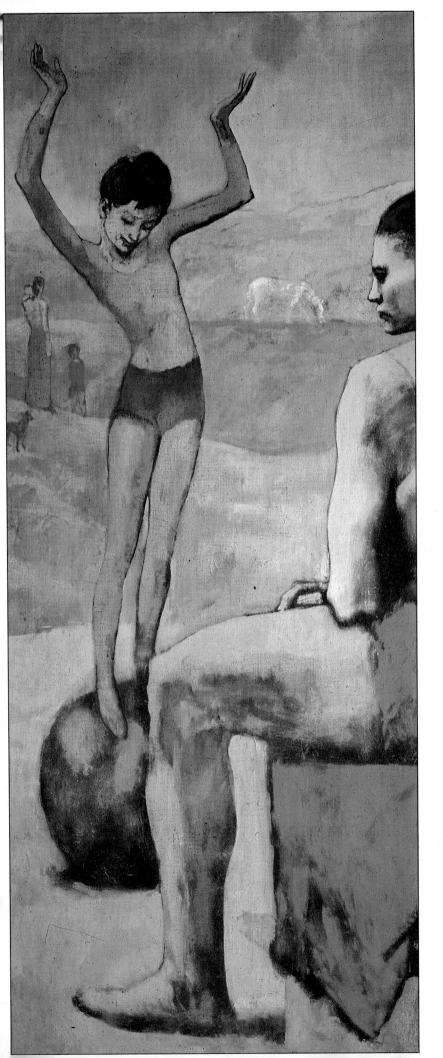

Important events in the life of

Pablo Picasso

1881   Picasso is born in Málaga, Spain on October 25.

1900   One of Picasso's paintings is chosen for the Spanish exhibit at the World Exhibition in Paris, and he makes his first journey there.

1901   Picasso begins his Blue Period paintings, which feature the poor people of Paris and Barcelona.

1904   He moves to Paris permanently and rents a studio in Montmartre.

1905   He begins his Rose Period paintings, which feature actors and circus performers.

1906–07   Picasso paints *Les Demoiselles d'Avignon*. He is influenced by art from other parts of the world.

1908   He begins working with Georges Braque to develop a new style of painting called Cubism.

1917–23   Picasso is influenced by ancient Greek and Roman art and paints in a neo-classical style.

1931   Picasso moves south of Paris and sets up a sculpture studio and printing workshop.

1937   He paints *Guernica* as a protest against the Spanish Civil War.

1947   He begins work on ceramics at Vallauris in the south of France.

1961   He marries for the second time and lives out of the public eye.

1973   Pablo Picasso dies on April 8.

ART FOR YOUNG PEOPLE

Pablo
Picasso

Matthew
Meadows

STERLING PUBLISHING CO., INC.   NEW YORK

Guernica, 1937

This is a detail from Pablo Picasso's most famous painting. Many people think it is one of the greatest paintings in the world. Picasso wanted everyone who saw the painting to feel the suffering of people in wartime. Guernica was a town in Spain which was bombed during the Spanish Civil War. Picasso didn't like to explain his paintings but he once said that the horse in the painting represents people and that the bull represents any kind of brutality in the world, not just the brutality of those who ordered the bombing of Guernica.

Cover: Portrait of Dora Maar, 1937

Page 2: detail from Young Acrobat on a Ball, 1905

Paintings in this book are identified by their title followed by the artist who painted them. If no artist is named the painting is by Pablo Picasso.

This book was prepared for Macdonald Young Books Ltd by Tucker Slingsby Creative Services London House 66–68 Upper Richmond Road London SW15 2RP

Project Editor: Katie Preston
Picture Researcher: Liz Eddison
Design concept by M&M Design Partnership
Designer: Steve Rowling
Artwork: George Fryer, Bernard Thornton Artists

Consultant: Tom Parsons

Subject Adviser:
Professor Arthur Hughes
Department of Art, University of Central England, Birmingham

Printed and bound in Portugal.
Sterling ISBN 0–8069–6160–0

Library of Congress Cataloging-in-Publication Data Available

1 2 3 4 5 6 7 8 9 10

Published in 1996 by Sterling Publishing Company, Inc 387 Park Avenue South New York, N.Y. 10016

Originally published in Great Britain by Macdonald Young Books Ltd, under the title *An Introduction to Pablo Picasso*

© 1996 Macdonald Young Books Ltd

Distributed in Canada by Sterling Publishing
c/o Canadian Manda Group,
One Atlantic Avenue, Suite 105
Toronto, Ontario, Canada M6K 3E7

Acknowledgements
The works of Pablo Picasso are © Succession Picasso/DACS 1996
l = left; r = right; t = top; b = bottom
Bridgeman Art Library: Front Cover:

Giraudon/Musée Picasso; Front End Paper: Pushkin Museum, Moscow; Title Page: Philadelphia Museum of Art; Prado, Madrid 4, 20–21b, 21tr, 29t; Musée Picasso 6, 7, 16, 19, 29b; Philadelphia Museum of Art 8; Pushkin Museum, Moscow 9l, 12; Cleveland Museum of Art, Ohio 9r; National Gallery of Scotland 11; Christie's London 14, 18; Tate Gallery, London 17t; Private Collection 17b; Redfern Gallery, London 24; Museo Nacional de Ceramica, Valencia 25; Hermitage, St Petersburg 26; Private Collection 27; Magyar Nemzeti Galeria, Budapest 28.

The Museum of Modern Art, New York 10.

Musée Picasso/Réunion des Musées Nationaux 13t,b, 15l,r, 22,23.

Hulton Deutsch 24t

A catalogue record for this book is available from the British Library

Contents

Growing up

Picasso is probably the most famous artist that ever lived. He was also one of the most creative, inventive and influential artists.

Pablo Picasso was born in Málaga, on the south coast of Spain, on October 25, 1881. He had two younger sisters named Lola and Conchita. His father, José Ruiz Blasco, was an art teacher and artist. He wanted Pablo to be an artist too—a more successful one than he had been.

By the time he was in his early teens, Pablo showed he had a great talent for drawing. His mother, Maria Picasso Lopez, said that Pablo's first word was "piz"—short for the Spanish word *lapiz*, which means pencil. When Pablo was ten years old, his father got a job at an art school in La Coruña in northern Spain. Pablo went to drawing classes at the school and learned painting at home with his father.

◄ **The Artist's Father, 1896**
Many of Picasso's earliest paintings are portraits of his family and friends. This watercolor was painted when Picasso was only fifteen and shows that he was already a talented artist.

▶ Sketch for Science and Charity, 1897
When he was sixteen, Picasso won a gold medal in a national art competition for the oil painting based on this sketch. Two years earlier, his youngest sister Conchita had died from a disease called diphtheria and the picture was partly based on his memories of her death.

The family moved to Barcelona in 1895. Pablo started going to art school there in 1897, but the school persuaded him to apply for the San Fernando Academy of Art in Madrid.

The family needed the help of a rich uncle to pay the academy's fees. They all wanted the boy to be a good, traditional Spanish artist, but Pablo had other ideas. After a few months he left the academy and returned home. To show his new independence, Pablo began to sign his pictures with his mother's middle name—Picasso.

Barcelona in the 1890s was a livelier and more modern city than Madrid.

■ *This picture shows a doctor and a nun by the bed of a dying woman. It is roughly and messily painted. Picasso based a larger, more finished painting on this sketch.*

Picasso met other artists at a café called *Els Quatre Gats* (The Four Cats). The artists called themselves "Modernistes" and talked about the exciting new art and ideas from other European cities, especially from Paris.

In 1899 one of Picasso's paintings, *Last Moments*, which was a deathbed scene like *Science and Charity*, was chosen for the Spanish Pavilion at the 1900 World Exhibition in Paris. Picasso decided to make his first visit to Paris.

First French steps

Picasso travelled to Paris in 1900 with an artist friend named Casegemas and they met up with other Spanish artists who had moved to Paris. Picasso brought with him some pastel drawings of Spanish bullfights and flamenco dancers. One or two art dealers started to sell his work, but Picasso and his friends were very poor.

Picasso moved back and forth between Barcelona and Paris for the next four years. He started experimenting with different painting styles and subjects.

At first he was influenced by French artists like Henri de Toulouse-Lautrec who painted bright pictures showing modern city life. Picasso began to draw and paint people having fun at cafés and dancehalls.

But as he began to look at city life in both Paris and Barcelona, Picasso saw many unhappy and poor people who were outcasts from society. He decided to show people's unhappiness in his paintings and began to paint portraits of beggars and other poor people.

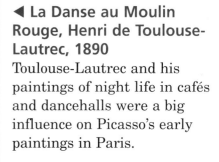

◀ **La Danse au Moulin Rouge, Henri de Toulouse-Lautrec, 1890**
Toulouse-Lautrec and his paintings of night life in cafés and dancehalls were a big influence on Picasso's early paintings in Paris.

■ *Toulouse-Lautrec's paintings were unusual because he used large areas of pure, flat color. This was a style he borrowed from Japanese art and from advertising posters, in Paris. In some of his early pictures, Picasso did the same.*

These are called "Blue Period" paintings because he used mainly blue and green to add to the sad mood.

In 1904 Picasso settled in Paris for good. He rented a studio called the Bateau-lavoir in Montmartre. In 1905 Picasso's work began to change. He started going to the Médrano Circus near his studio and began painting the acrobats and clowns. These pictures used warm, rosy tones and come from the "Rose Period" of Picasso's work.

▲ **La Vie, 1903**
"The Life" is one of Picasso's Blue Period paintings. He used the face of his friend Casegemas, who died in 1901, as a model for the man in the painting. Picasso was so poor when he painted this picture he could not afford to buy new materials. He painted over the *Last Moments* canvas, which had been picked for the 1900 World Exhibition.

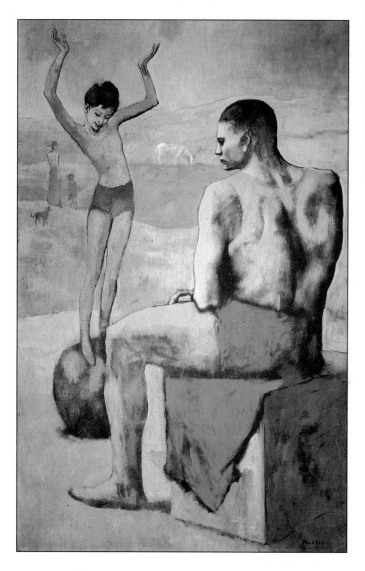

◀ **Young Acrobat on a Ball, 1905**
As Picasso began to feel happier, his paintings looked happier too. He started using warm, pink colors instead of cold blues and greens and he began painting happier subjects, like these circus performers. In some ways the circus people were outcasts from society too, but they were not victims—they chose to live this way.

Start of modern art

Ideas about art were changing rapidly in the early 1900s. Traditionally, artists were supposed to make their paintings perfect copies of the subject. They were also meant to make people and things look beautiful. To artists such as Picasso, who could draw brilliantly by the age of sixteen, this was not a challenge. The challenge was to create something new.

▶ **African mask**
Halfway through painting *Les Demoiselles d'Avignon*, Picasso went to see an exhibition of African art including tribal masks. He liked them so much that he made two faces in the painting look like African tribal masks.

▶ **Les Demoiselles d'Avignon, 1906–07**
Picasso shocked the art world with this painting of "The Ladies of Avignon" because it is not a "realistic" picture and because the women do not look beautiful.

■ *Picasso worked on this picture on and off for about a year. He wanted to paint a traditional subject in a new way. All the old rules have been broken: the faces of the two women on the right are like African masks; the woman in the corner has her back to us, but her head is facing us.*

► **Three Tahitians, Paul Gauguin, 1899**
Like Picasso, Gauguin was influenced by art from other cultures. He not only painted pictures of the Tahitian people, he also learned painting techniques from Tahitian craftsmen and used them in his paintings.

In about 1905, a new group of artists appeared. They painted strong pictures with bright, unmixed colors, often squeezing their paint tubes straight onto the canvas. They decorated their pictures with such strong patterns that they were soon nicknamed the Fauves, which means "wild animals" in French. Their leader was Henri Matisse, who was Picasso's great rival.

Picasso did not follow this group of painters, but he did begin experimenting with new ways to show the human body. He was inspired by an exhibition of Iron Age stone sculpture. He copied the roughly carved figures in his paintings of naked bodies.

Picasso made the bodies thick and heavy and built up the figures out of simple shapes which he outlined in black. Picasso was also influenced by an exhibition of work by Paul Gauguin in 1906. Gauguin was inspired by art from other parts of the world and had spent several years living on the island of Tahiti in the Pacific Ocean.

In 1907 Picasso painted a picture called *Les Demoiselles d'Avignon*. The women in the picture are posed like models, but even Picasso's friends were shocked by how ugly they looked. This picture is different from any painted before and many people say it marks the beginning of modern art.

Cubes and cardboard

In 1908, with his friend Georges Braque, Picasso began developing a new style of painting called Cubism. They were inspired by the painter Paul Cézanne. He was the first artist to break the old rules of painting. He did not want to create illusions of reality with paintings and did not try to paint exact copies of things.

In some pictures, Cézanne combined information about an object taken from several different viewpoints and at different times. The Cubists took this idea further and tried to show all sides of an object in one picture. They turned the front and sides of objects they painted into a pattern of flat shapes. Objects look as though they are being seen through a broken mirror.

As Cubism developed, it became harder to recognize the people and objects in the paintings because the images became even more broken up, with the bits re-arranged all over the place. Braque and Picasso stuck to painting everyday objects, like bottles, newspapers and musical instruments. We need fewer clues to help us recognize these things.

◄ **Portrait of Ambroise Vollard, 1909–10**
This is a Cubist painting of Ambroise Vollard, who was Picasso's art dealer in Paris from when the artist was only nineteen. The painting is very inventive. Although Vollard's face has been turned into groups of triangular shapes, it is still recognizable. A year or so later Picasso's "portraits" rarely resembled his models at all.

Braque taught Picasso how to imitate marble and wood in his paintings. They went on to stick real wood, as well as wood-pattern paper, cloth, string and other materials, onto their pictures.

▶ Cardboard Guitar, 1912
These cardboard "constructions" were the start of modern sculpture.

▲ Violin and Sheet of Music, 1912
Picasso cut shapes out of colored paper and stuck the pieces on top of each other to make his collages. He also added bits of "real" objects, such as newspapers and sheets of music.

The rhythm and energy of the pictures reflected the pace of modern city life. The Cubists called them "collages," from the French word *coller*, which means "to stick." Collage became the most important art invention of the twentieth century. Picasso went on to make solid Cubist still lifes using materials such as cardboard, tin and bits of rubbish. This was a totally new way to make sculptures.

ster of style

◄ **The Coffee Pot, about 1940**
This later still life looks more like the Cubist painting on page 12. The objects are made up of flat shapes like squares and triangles and they are seen from a strange viewpoint.

Until Picasso, most artists developed one style they liked and stuck to it. Picasso kept changing his style and inventing new ways of making art. He said, "Whenever I had something to say, I have said it in the manner in which I have felt it ought to be said." Although the styles he used were modern, the subjects, such as still lifes and portraits, were traditional ones.

Picasso gave up doing Cubist collages and sculptures in 1917. He did not want to be labeled as belonging to a particular group of artists. He started working in several different styles. Some of these he copied and borrowed from other artists, alive and dead. He liked to say "If there is something to be stolen, I shall steal it."

In the 1920s, when he was in his forties, Picasso was well on his way to becoming the most famous artist of the twentieth century. Many of his exhibitions were held outside France, and this made him even more famous. Inventions like cinema, air travel and the radio meant news traveled quickly, and Picasso was always happy to be interviewed and photographed.

From the age of thirty Picasso did not have to worry about money. At forty he was very wealthy and at sixty-five he was a millionaire. Just after World War II, he bought a house in France. He paid for it with one still life painting.

▶ **Still Life with Pitcher and Apples, 1919**
Like other artists after World War I, which ended in 1918, Picasso's work for a time was less experimental. Pictures from this period describe the world in a more recognizable way. This style was called neo-classical because the people and objects in the pictures looked heavy and solid, like the stone sculptures from the "classical age" of ancient Greece and Rome.

◀ **Large Still Life on a Pedestal Table, 1931**
The strong, curved lines in this painting make it look rather like a cartoon.

■ *In this still life Picasso has outlined the different objects with thick black lines and then filled in the spaces these make with bright, clear colors. As a result the picture resembles the stained glass windows you see in churches. The colors and shapes are full of energy and life. Picasso must have liked this painting. He kept it for himself and did not sell it.*

Models, mothers and families

Picasso lived with many women throughout his life and had four children. They all modeled for his paintings, prints and sculptures. It was said that when he changed girlfriends he changed his style of painting too.

Picasso's first girlfriend in Paris was a young woman called Fernande Olivier.

She lived above his Bateau-lavoir studio. In 1912 Picasso started going out with Eva Gouel. When she died in 1916, he was very sad. He met his first wife, Olga, on a trip to Rome later that year. They had a son named Paul in 1921. In 1927 Picasso started having an affair with a young model named Marie-Therèse Walter. Picasso was said to have loved her more than any other woman. They had a daughter named Maia in 1935.

When she found out about Maia, Olga left, taking Paul with her. Picasso's next affair was with a photographer and reporter named Dora Maar. She was a clever woman and liked discussing Picasso's paintings with him.

In 1943 Picasso met Françoise Gilot. They lived together and had a son named Claude and a daughter named Paloma. He met Jacqueline Roque in 1954 and married her in 1961.

◀ **Olga in an Armchair, 1917**
Picasso painted this beautiful portrait of his first wife, Olga Koklova, from a photograph he had taken of her. The painting of the figure is very detailed, but Picasso has left the background unfinished.

◀ Weeping Woman (Dora Maar), 1937

Dora Maar was another important woman in Picasso's life. She was a photographer from Yugoslavia who knew lots of artists in Paris and took a great interest in Picasso's work. She was friends with a group of painters called the Surrealists. They painted strange, dream-like paintings, which did not bear any resemblance to reality. She introduced Picasso to their ideas.

■ *In this portrait Picasso shows Dora's weeping face side and front together, with black and white teeth and fingers. He painted her not long after finishing his black-and-white anti-war painting, Guernica (page 20), which shows several weeping women. When asked about her portrait, he said Dora was always crying.*

Picasso enjoyed family life but his art always came first. He drew and painted children all his life. He said he wanted to draw like a child too, but never could, even when he was a boy.

In many of his portraits of women, Picasso changed their shapes so much it is hard to recognize them as people. He liked the idea of making them look strange or dream-like and so more interesting. Sometimes the distortions look cruel, as in the portrait of Dora.

▶ Portrait of Jacqueline, 1954

Jacqueline, Picasso's second wife, was one of his favorite subjects later in his life. In fact, in just one year (1963) he painted 150 portraits of her.

Beside the seaside

Perhaps because he had been brought up by the sea, Picasso loved the seaside. The beach was a place to have fun and play, particularly on family holidays. After moving to France, he went on holiday to the Mediterranean in the south or to the Atlantic coast in the west.

In the 1940s, he moved to the south of France. He was often photographed on the beach at holiday resorts like Juan les Pins. Because he was famous he helped make these towns popular.

Dinard

Paris

Atlantic Ocean

Biarritz

Juan les Pins

Mediterranean Sea

◀ **Baigneuse, about 1925**
Over the years Picasso painted lots of beach scenes: pictures of people playing or lazing about, posed against a simple background of sand and sea.

■ *The body of this bather is large and solid but there is a stillness about her. These were qualities Picasso admired in classical Roman and Greek sculpture.*

▶ The Bathers, 1918
In 1918 Picasso went on honeymoon to Biarritz with his first wife Olga. This is where he painted these bathing beauties in their old-fashioned swimsuits.

■ *Compared to the bathing figure opposite, the women in this picture seem to have rather strange bodies. They appear a little elongated, their limbs curling with playful energy. Picasso was having fun with this painting. This was a picture he kept for himself and never sold.*

Picasso enjoyed painting at the seaside and put elements from the beach into his paintings. Sometimes he mixed sand into his paint, which gave it a rough texture. Sometimes he made collages from bits and pieces he found on the beach, such as driftwood, cork or rope. He also painted shapes with glue and sprinkled over sand, just as you put glitter on Christmas cards.

Picasso went back to ideas and subjects again and again. In August 1928, he went to Dinard in Brittany for a holiday with Olga and Paul. There he made several small paintings of funny flat figures with arms and legs in the wrong places. Nearly 30 years later he made a group of similar figures from scraps of wood which he also called *The Bathers*.

War paintings

Picasso lived through World War I (1914–18) and World War II (1939–45). Spain didn't take part in either of these wars, so Picasso was "neutral" and spent most of both wars in Paris and carried on painting.

In 1916, his friend Jean Cocteau persuaded him to come to Rome to design scenery and costumes for a Russian ballet company. This is where he met his first wife Olga.

The ballet, *Parade*, was booed when it opened back in Paris the following year. Picasso had made the costumes surreal and strange. Some characters wore cardboard sculptures of buildings and trees on their heads, which made them massively tall. Because the war was being fought just 150 miles away, the audience thought the ballet should have been more patriotic to France and that Picasso's modern designs weren't serious enough.

When war broke out in Spain in 1936, Picasso did take sides; he supported the Republicans against the dictator General Franco. When planes bombed the village of Guernica in April 1937, Picasso began working on a painting to protest against the bombing. The picture, called *Guernica*, was shown at the Spanish Pavilion at the 1937 World Exhibition in Paris.

Picasso did not paint the actual scene of the bombing, but wanted to show the terrible things people suffer during wartime. He showed war from the victim's point of view.

▲ **Sketch for Guernica, 1937**
Guernica is a very large painting—it measures over 11 feet high by over 25 feet wide. Picasso did lots of sketches for the different elements of the painting before putting them together.

Picasso had used all the ideas in *Guernica* before—distorted figures with legs and arms at strange angles, weeping women and animals. Now they all came together in a new way, with a meaning that everyone who saw the painting understood. *Guernica* made Picasso world famous and many people think it is his greatest painting.

◄ **Guernica, 1937**
This painting tells the story of the bombing without showing the event itself. The bomb is only hinted at in the flash of the electric bulb and a flare of light above a door.

Heavy metal

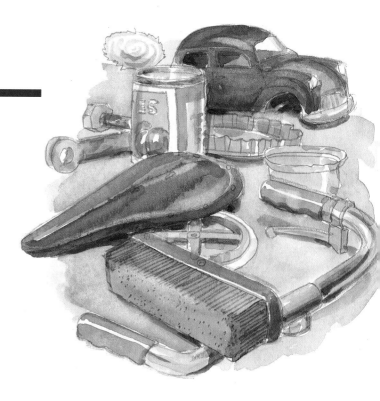

Picasso made sculptures on and off throughout his long life. He showed that sculptures can be made from any material you like, but you need to use different techniques for each different material. For example, steel must be cut and the pieces bent or welded together. Picasso was very quick at learning these new skills. And each time he did, he found a new way to use them.

In 1924 he did some spiky drawings to illustrate a book. He wanted to make solid "drawings" in thick wire from the illustrations and asked a sculptor friend to help.

▲ Objets trouvés
This phrase is French for "found objects." Picasso created sculptures from collections of everyday objects just like this.

▶ Bull's Head, 1943
This is a very simple metal sculpture. Picasso assembled the head of a bull out of the saddle of a bicycle and a set of handlebars. The original components have not been altered at all but it looks like a bull's head, not a bike.

Julio Gonzalez was also Spanish and living in France. In 1928 he taught Picasso how to weld and then worked with him for nearly two years.

Picasso loved junk. He often visited junk yards to see what he could pick up there. He said he saw the two parts that made up the *Bull's Head* next to each other in a heap of junk.

Picasso knew immediately that he could turn the handlebars and bicycle saddle into a sculpture. Both the cardboard Cubist sculptures (see page 13) and the metal sculptures like the *Bull's Head* are made with *objets trouvés*, which means "found objects."

The cardboard ones are called "constructions" because Picasso built the sculpture by folding, gluing and painting the original materials. The metal sculptures like the bull are called "assemblages" because Picasso simply assembled the sculpture without altering the original materials.

In his seventies and eighties, Picasso created cut-outs from paper and cardboard that were made up in metal with the help of a neighbor who owned a metal factory. Picasso also teamed up with a sculptor who sand-blasted Picasso's designs onto enormous slabs of concrete.

In the past, most metal sculpture was cast. The sculptor would make a model in clay and then use it to make a mold. Molten metal was poured into the mold to make the finished sculpture. Picasso broke with this tradition and used other techniques, such as welding, that had not been used for art before.

◀ **The Footballer, 1961**
Picasso was eighty when he made this 5-yard-high sculpture showing a soccer player in action. He first made a small version of the sculpture from cut paper and cardboard, then this large version was made from sheets of metal.

23

Pots and plates

When Picasso was in his late sixties, just after World War II, he became interested in ceramics, which means pottery plates, vases and bowls. He started to work in a pottery in Vallauris owned by a couple named Mr. and Mrs. Ramié.

▲ Ceramics exhibition
In 1948 Picasso exhibited several of his pots and plates at a pottery and ceramics exhibition at La Maison de la Pensée Français in Paris, France.

◀ Clockwise from top left: Face, 1969; Owl and Profiles, Head of a Faun, Pitcher with Heads, Owl, Fish on a White Background, 1952; Three Fishes, 1947; Head of a Faun, 1948.
When Picasso first worked with clay, he only decorated the surface of the jugs and plates, as he has done here. Later, he started experimenting with making shapes out of the clay, which was more like making sculpture than pottery.

▶ Majolica Plate, about 1950
Sometimes Picasso scratched designs into the plate or bowl to add texture before adding color using special pottery glazes. Here he has made the plate into a face.

Vallauris was just outside Cannes in the south of France. Ceramics had been made there since Roman times, but local potteries could no longer compete with the new cheap plastic and aluminum crockery being produced by factories.

At first Picasso simply decorated the pots, plates and tiles made by the Ramiés. Picasso used the shape as the starting point for his decorative ideas: the jugs became figures, the plates became faces or scenes of bullfights with the crowds painted around the rim.

Later, Picasso wanted to work with the clay itself, not just decorate it. He pinched, stretched and squeezed the shapes the local potters made for him, cutting bits off one piece and sticking them on to another, then scratching designs into the clay.

Picasso's ceramics sometimes featured strange mixtures of animals and people, like the mythical faun (half man, half goat) and centaur (half horse, half man). Many of his ideas came from ancient Roman ceramics.

Picasso stayed near Vallauris for ten years, making the town famous for its pottery again. The locals celebrated his birthday with a festival, and a bullfight was held in his honor.

25

Drawing and printmaking

Picasso worked in lots of different mediums—clay, metal, paper, oil paints, pastels. Whatever medium he was using, his ideas always started from drawings. He tried out different ways of doing something in pencil first to see what worked best. Of course this is true of most artists. They fill sketch books with drawings and sketches of the things that interest them most.

A lot of Picasso's art is graphic, which means "drawn." He would draw the outlines of a picture and then fill in the shapes with color. Often the paintings seem unfinished because he left bits of the drawing uncovered (see the portrait on page 16). For Picasso, the drawing part was as important as the painting part. Many of his paintings look like patterns of lines filled in with color, which is why they look so flat.

A print is made by drawing or etching a picture on a plate (a block, stone or sheet). Then ink or color is added and the design is printed on to paper.

◀ **Woman in a Hat, 1963**
This is a type of print called a color linocut. The woman is probably Picasso's wife, Jacqueline.

■ **Making a linocut**
Lino is a thin piece of tough plastic glued on to a heavy canvas backing. To make a linocut print, a drawing is first done on a piece of lino (1), then the design is cut with special tools (2). The surface of the lino is covered with ink (3) and paper is pressed down to make a print (4).

◀ **Satyrs and Goats, 1959**
This is another linocut. Satyrs were goat-like men from Greek legends. Picasso often looked to ancient Greece and Rome for inspiration for his paintings, pottery, sculpture and prints.

It's not surprising that Picasso liked printmaking so much, because it meant he had new ways of drawing lines and filling in areas of color. He drew his designs on copper plates and soft stones and found exciting ways to create pictures. He loved working with skilled craftspeople, such as potters and printers, and learning their techniques.

In 1959, when he was seventy-seven, Picasso discovered linocut prints. In this method, the drawing is cut out of a floor covering called linoleum. Over the next four years he made more than 300 linocuts. He made posters for his pottery exhibitions at Vallauris, adapting the ceramic designs he had created there.

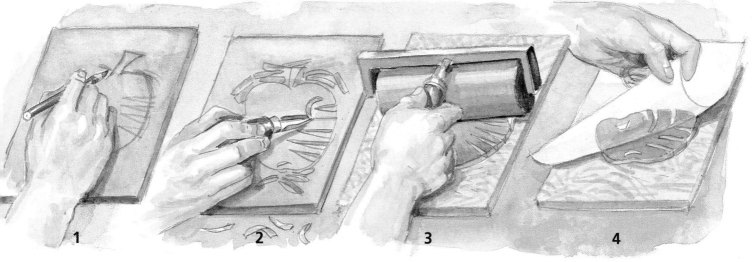

1   2   3   4

27

A ripe old age

By the 1950s, Picasso was the most famous and popular artist in the world. He had been given many international prizes and exhibitions. These showed artworks from all stages of his long career. Despite this, he was no longer part of the modern art scene in Europe and America. Most artists there saw him as a bit old-fashioned. But his work was still influential in other parts of the world, especially India, where people were attracted to Picasso's flat, decorative styles.

During his last 20 years, Picasso worked faster and faster, producing many different kinds of work. He did his own versions of famous pictures by past great European artists, like the Spanish artist Velazquez, almost as if he were challenging them.

From 1963 onward he worked mainly in his studio at his large home in the hills above Cannes. This was partly because of old age and partly because he was so famous he could not walk anywhere without being surrounded by people.

These later pictures look sloppy and unfinished, partly because Picasso did them so quickly. Picasso himself said, "Completing something means killing it, depriving it of life and soul." He was an old man trying to keep death at bay with his art. He died, at the age of ninety-one, on April 8, 1973.

◀ **Musketeer with a Sword, 1972**
This is a self-portrait of Picasso aged eighty-nine. He painted himself as one of *The Three Musketeers* which was his favorite TV program.

▶ Las Meniñas, Velazquez, 1656

Velazquez was a great Spanish artist whom Picasso had studied at art school. At the end of his life, Picasso decided to do his own version of one of Velazquez' greatest works.

▼ Las Meniñas, 1957

Picasso worked on his versions of Velazquez' *Las Meniñas* (The Maidens) from August 17 to December 30, 1957. He studied the original closely and did lots of paintings and drawings based on it in his own style. He kept the basic composition and the lighting but changed other elements. The boy on the right, for example, is holding his hands out in front of him in the original, so Picasso painted in a piano for him to play.

More Information

Glossary

collage A picture made by sticking paper, cardboard, cloth or other materials onto a surface.

composition The way in which the different parts of a picture are arranged.

Cubism A style of painting in which the artist tries to show all sides of an object at once.

distortion Changing the usual shape of an object.

neo-classical Means "new classical." It describes a style that copies or takes ideas from the art of ancient Greece or Rome.

oil paint Type of paint where colors are mixed with oil (usually linseed). It is sold in tubes.

objets trouvés Means "found objects." Artists, particularly Picasso and the Surrealists, used everyday objects, such as newspapers and cardboard, in their work.

pastels Art crayons made from powdered paints stuck together with gum.

political painting Painting that has a message about what governments and leaders are doing.

Republicans The left-wing party in Spain, who were elected by the people to govern the country. They were defeated by the Fascists in the Spanish Civil War.

Spanish Civil War A war in Spain between 1936 and 1939, in which the Fascists led by General Franco defeated the Republicans. Many people were killed.

still life A painting or drawing of objects, such as fruit, vases, flowers, etc.

Surrealists Artists who painted or sculpted strange images from their imagination. Sometimes they painted dreamlike scenes or put together strange combinations of objects in a painting or sculpture.

watercolor A kind of paint that can be mixed with water.

welding A way of joining pieces of metal together, by heating them.

World War I A war fought between 1914 and 1918, mostly in Europe.

World War II A war fought between 1939 and 1945 in Europe, Africa and Asia.

People

Georges Braque 1882-1963. French painter who, with Picasso, started the Cubist style of painting.

Paul Cézanne 1839-1906. French painter who worked in a new style. Often called the founder of modern art.

Jean Cocteau 1889-1963. French poet, playwright and film director.

General Franco 1892-1975. Dictator of Spain from 1939 to 1975.

Paul Gauguin 1848-1903. French artist who worked in strong colors and bold outlines. He went to live on the Pacific island of Tahiti.

Henri Matisse 1869-1954. Painter and sculptor and leading member of the Fauve group of artists. He was Picasso's greatest rival.

Henri de Toulouse-Lautrec 1864-1901. French painter and graphic artist. Best known for his pictures of Paris dance halls, cafés and entertainers.

Diego Rodriguez Velazquez 1599-1660. A great Spanish painter of the 17th century, who was court painter to the Spanish royal family.

Index